KU-131-959

CONTENTS

THE MOVING EARTH   4

VOLCANOES   10

TYPES OF VOLCANO   14

LIVING WITH VOLCANOES   16

EARTHQUAKES   20

EFFECTS OF EARTHQUAKES   24

TSUNAMIS AND MUDFLOWS   28

GLOSSARY   30

FURTHER INFORMATION   31

INDEX   32

THE MOVING EARTH

Earth's surface is always changing. Many of these changes take place slowly. For example, rocks on Earth's surface are slowly broken apart through the process of **weathering**. **Erosion** may then move these rock pieces to new places.

Some changes on Earth's surface happen quickly.

Volcanoes and earthquakes are two events that can bring changes to an area within minutes.

A volcanic **eruption** can send out showers of hot ash, rocks, streams of molten **lava** and boiling hot gases. An eruption can quickly kill and clear away all the plants in an area. In built-up areas, an eruption can cover houses and even whole towns so that they disappear.

DISCOVERING GEOGRAPHY

VOLCANOES AND EARTHQUAKES

Rebecca Hunter

Raintree

www.raintreepublishers.co.uk
Visit our website to find out more information about **Raintree** books.

To order:
☎ Phone 44 (0) 1865 888112
 Send a fax to 44 (0) 1865 314091
💻 Visit the Raintree Bookshop at **www.raintreepublishers.co.uk** to browse our catalogue and order online.

First published in Great Britain by Raintree,
Halley Court, Jordan Hill, Oxford
OX2 8EJ, part of Harcourt Education.

Raintree is a registered trademark of Harcourt Education Ltd.

Produced for Raintree by Discovery Books Ltd
Design: Ian Winton
Editorial: Rebecca Hunter
Consultant: Jeremy Bloomfield
Commissioned photography: Chris Fairclough
Illustrations: Keith Williams, Stefan Chabluk and Pamela Goodchild
Production: Jonathan Smith

Originated by Dot Gradations Ltd
Printed and bound in China by South China Printing Company

ISBN 1 844 21681 0 (hardback)
07 06 05 04 03
10 9 8 7 6 5 4 3 2 1

ISBN 1 844 21686 1 (paperback)
08 07 06 05 04
10 9 8 7 6 5 4 3 2 1

British Library Cataloguing in Publication Data
Hunter, Rebecca
Volcanoes and Earthquakes. – (Discovering Geography)
551.2'1
A full catalogue record for this book is available from the British Library.

Acknowledgements
The publishers would like to thank the following for permission to reproduce photographs:
Bruce Coleman pp. **15** bottom (Jeff Foott), **16**; Corbis pp. **5** top, **13**, **19** top (Bob Krist), **21**, **28**, **29**; Getty Images pp. **4** (Glen Allison), **12** (G Brad Lewis), **14**, **15** top (Oliver Strewe), **17** bottom (Nicholas DeVore), **18** Thomas Brase), **19** bottom (Dave Saunders), **20** (James Balog); NASA p. **6**; Oxford Scientific Films pp. **5** bottom (Dieter and Mary Plage), **9** (Rick Price), **25** (Warren   (Simon Gilliam); Science Photo   son).

           cano reproduced with permission   (Simon Fraser).

           e to thank the following schools   equipment, models and   sessions: Bedstone College,   llow and Packwood Haugh, Shrewsbury.

Every effort has been made to contact copyright holders of any material reproduced in this book.
Any omissions will be rectified in subsequent printings if notice is given to the publishers.

Any words appearing in the text in bold, **like this**, are explained in the Glossary.

An earthquake is a shaking of the ground caused by movements beneath Earth's surface. Strong earthquakes can collapse buildings, bridges and other structures and destroy a city in seconds.

▶ *An artist paints in the ruins of a building after an earthquake in San Francisco, USA, in 1906.*

Volcanoes and earthquakes are two of the most frightening and dangerous events on Earth.

We cannot control the forces under the ground, but we can understand why they happen if we look deep inside Earth itself.

◀ *Just before a volcano erupts, it throws out huge clouds of dust and gas.*

STRUCTURE OF EARTH

Earth is made up of several layers of rock and metal.
Some of these are solid and some are liquid.

The centre of Earth is called the **core**. The core is
very hot, probably about 5000 °Celsius. The inner
part of the core is solid and is made of the metals iron
and nickel. The outer part of the core is made of
liquid iron.

Outside the core is a layer called the **mantle**. The mantle is made of rocks so hot that some are molten (melted into liquid). Molten rock is called **magma** and its temperature is about 800 °Celsius.

The outside layer of Earth is called the **crust**. This is the part we live on. The crust is made of solid rock and is like a skin over Earth.

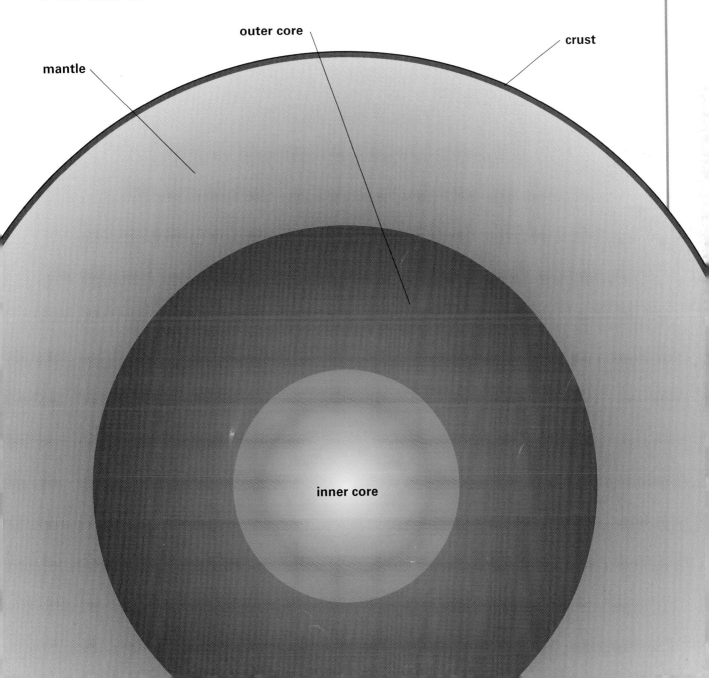

VOLCANO AND EARTHQUAKE ZONES

Earth's **crust** is made up of huge pieces that fit together like a giant jigsaw puzzle. These pieces are called **plates**. Some plates carry whole continents on them, such as the North American plate. Other plates form huge areas of the ocean floor.

The edges of plates, where they rub together, is where you are most likely to find volcanoes and earthquakes. An area in the Pacific Ocean that is dotted with volcanoes is known as the 'Ring of Fire'. Three-quarters of the world's earthquakes also occur in this zone.

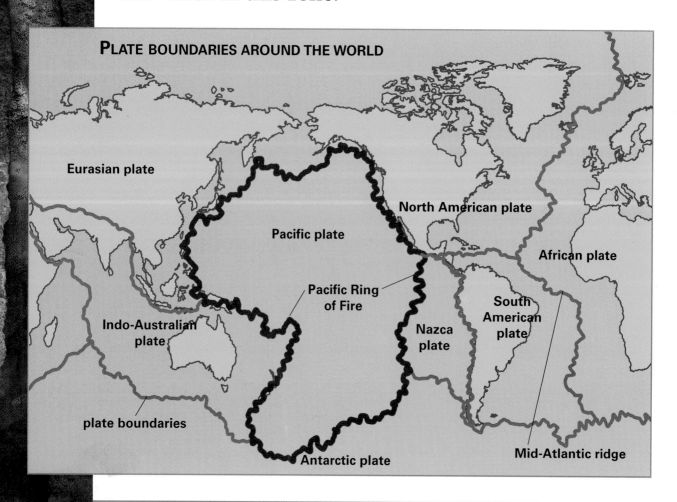

PLATE BOUNDARIES AROUND THE WORLD

Eurasian plate

North American plate

Pacific plate

African plate

Pacific Ring of Fire

South American plate

Indo-Australian plate

Nazca plate

plate boundaries

Mid-Atlantic ridge

Antarctic plate

MOUNTAIN BUILDING

Earth's plates are moving very slowly all the time. When two plates are pushed together, one plate will rise up above the other. This is how some kinds of mountains are formed.

MOVING CONTINENTS
We do not usually notice the movement of plates, but it can be measured. Western Europe is moving away from North America by about 2.5 centimetres each year.

The Andes mountains were formed over millions of years as the Nazca plate collided with the South American plate.

VOLCANOES

WHAT IS A VOLCANO?

Have you ever shaken a can of fizzy drink before opening it? When you do, the **pressure** in the can forces the liquid out in a messy explosion. The same kind of thing happens when a volcano **erupts**.

The hot, molten **magma** inside Earth is under great pressure, just like the drink in your can. If this pressure becomes too great, the magma will find its way out, making a violent explosion at the surface.

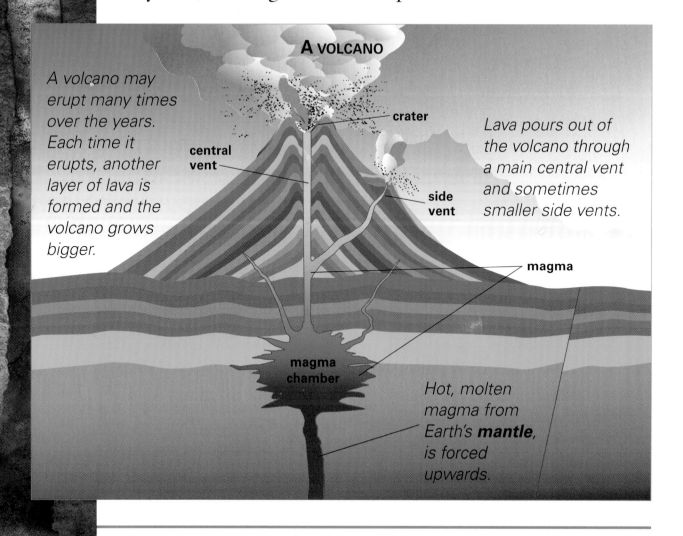

A VOLCANO

A volcano may erupt many times over the years. Each time it erupts, another layer of lava is formed and the volcano grows bigger.

central vent

crater

side vent

Lava pours out of the volcano through a main central vent and sometimes smaller side vents.

magma

magma chamber

Hot, molten magma from Earth's **mantle**, is forced upwards.

Once magma reaches Earth's surface it is called **lava**. During an eruption, red-hot lava, rocks and clouds of ash, steam and other gases, pour out creating a volcano.

PROJECT

Make your own volcano.

You will need:
a small plastic bottle
baking powder
vinegar
some sand or soil
a teaspoon
a tablespoon
a plastic funnel.

1. Put 2 teaspoons of baking powder in the plastic bottle, using the funnel.

2. Stand the bottle in the garden or on a table, and surround it by sand or soil to make the 'volcano'.

3. Add one tablespoon of vinegar, and watch the volcano erupt!

LAVA

Some **lava** can flow very fast. Other kinds of lava move slowly – at walking pace. Lava continues to flow from a volcano (like the one below) as long as there is enough **pressure** to force it to the surface.

DUST AND ASH

Volcanic dust and ash also move down the sides of a volcano. These materials are often more dangerous than lava. The **eruption** of Mount Pinatubo, in the Philippines, in 1991 buried much of the island of Luzon in ash.

CRATERS AND CALDERAS

Craters are the hollows that form in the opening at the top of volcanoes. Craters are usually quite small, about 1 kilometre (0.6 miles) in diameter. Calderas are very large craters formed by an explosion or a large volcanic eruption. Calderas are often more than 5 kilometres (3 miles) in diameter. The world's largest caldera is at Aso, Japan, and is 23 kilometres (14 miles) long and 16 kilometres (10 miles) wide.

This lake is in the crater of the Mount Pinatubo volcano on the island of Luzon, in the Philippines.

TYPES OF VOLCANO

There are three types of volcano. Volcanoes that still **erupt** regularly are called active volcanoes. There are about 500 active volcanoes in the world, a few of which erupt every year.

VOLCANIC TIME BOMB!

Mauna Loa in Hawaii, USA, is the world's largest active volcano. Mauna Loa has erupted 15 times since 1900. Its most recent eruption was in 1984, but it is certain to erupt again.

White Island volcano is one of New Zealand's most active volcanoes. It has erupted 35 times since 1826.

DORMANT VOLCANOES

Dormant, or 'sleeping', volcanoes are ones that are quiet for a long time and then suddenly erupt again. Mount Egmont in New Zealand has not erupted since 1755. It is a dormant volcano. No one knows when it may erupt again.

Mount Egmont, a dormant volcano in New Zealand.

EXTINCT VOLCANOES

A dormant volcano may become active again, or it may 'die' and become extinct. In an extinct volcano, the **magma** under the surface cools and becomes solid. Most extinct volcanoes have not erupted for thousands of years. Mount Kilimanjaro in Tanzania, and the Devil's Tower in Wyoming, USA, are both extinct volcanoes.

The Devil's Tower in Wyoming, USA, is the remains of an old, extinct volcano.

LIVING WITH VOLCANOES

L iving near a volcano is not something most of us would choose to do. Yet throughout history people have lived and worked on the slopes of volcanoes.

The island of Surtsey was formed off the coast of Iceland in 1963 by a volcanic eruption.

Volcanoes are one type of mountain-building force at work on Earth. If you look at a map of the world, many of the islands that you see dotted around the oceans are actually the remains of old volcanoes. More volcanoes are found underwater than on land. Most of these remain totally **submerged**, but sometimes, after many **eruptions**, a volcano grows larger and larger until it breaks through the surface and forms an island.

As early people explored the world, they crossed oceans using these volcanic islands as stops to refill their water and food supplies. Some explorers remained on the islands, starting farms and villages.

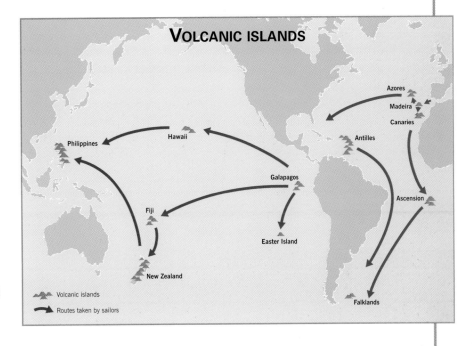

VOLCANIC ISLANDS

Azores
Madeira
Canaries
Antilles
Philippines
Hawaii
Galapagos
Ascension
Fiji
Easter Island
New Zealand
Falklands

Volcanic islands
Routes taken by sailors

Volcanic ash and **lava** eventually produce very fertile soils. They are rich in minerals that make plants grow especially well. This is why people are willing to risk living near volcanoes. They can grow good crops. Fruit trees and vines thrive on the slopes of Mount Etna in Sicily.

The town of Taormina in Sicily with Mount Etna behind.

USEFUL VOLCANOES

One useful side effect of volcanic activity is **geothermal** energy. This is the heat energy that naturally occurs deep inside Earth. In volcanic areas, geothermal energy may be near the surface of the ground in the form of hot springs. In some places hot water shoots out of the ground in a tall fountain called a geyser. Some geysers **erupt** very regularly.

Underground hot water can be used to generate electricity. In areas where there is no natural underground water, it is possible to pump water down into Earth to be heated, and then return it to the surface to be used.

Old Faithful in Yellowstone Park, USA, erupts about every 76 minutes with a spout of water up to 46 metres high.

A woman bakes bread using a geothermal oven in Iceland.

Over 20 countries now use geothermal energy. In Iceland, there is so much hot water available that people use it to heat their homes and greenhouses.

Old volcanoes are also useful as sources of precious metals and gemstones. The heat from volcanoes makes metals in the **crust** melt and flow through cracks in the rocks, where they cool and become solid. Gold, silver and copper are all found in old volcanoes.

A miner drills for gold in the Hartebeestfontein mine – an old volcano in South Africa.

EARTHQUAKES

Every 30 seconds an earthquake occurs somewhere in the world. Most of them cause no damage at all, but more than once each month a major earthquake occurs.

An earthquake, or **tremor**, is a shaking of the ground caused by movements of the **plates** of rock in Earth's **crust**. The plates slowly move and try to slide past each other. This causes an enormous amount of strain to build up. When the strain becomes too great, the rocks underground crack and shift. This sends out shock waves and produces an earthquake that makes the ground tremble at the surface.

At the San Andreas **fault** in California, USA, two plates are slowly sliding past each other. Many earthquakes happen along this fault line.

The San Andreas fault runs for 435 kilometres (270 miles) through central California, USA.

In 1906 a huge earthquake shook the city of San Francisco early in the morning. The earthquake lasted for 1 minute as the San Andreas fault moved about 6 metres. Many buildings were destroyed by the earthquake, but more by the fire that swept through the city afterwards. Nearly 8 square kilometres and more than 28,000 buildings were burned out. Many people were killed and thousands left homeless.

There was chaos in the streets of San Franciso after the earthquake in 1906.

In October 1989, another large earthquake shook San Francisco. Over 200 people were killed. Despite the risk of earthquakes, San Francisco is still a popular place to live.

MEASURING EARTHQUAKES

The centre of an earthquake, deep underground, is called the focus. Above this, on the surface of Earth, is

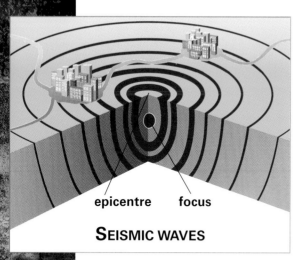

epicentre   focus

SEISMIC WAVES

the **epicentre**. Vibrations called **seismic waves** spread out from the focus in rings. The waves are strongest at the epicentre, and they get weaker as they spread out.

Scientists who study earthquakes are called seismologists. They use machines called seismographs to record the pattern of seismic waves and work out the strength of each earthquake.

Earthquakes are often measured on the Richter scale, which measures the energy released on a scale of 1–9.

RICHTER SCALE

Magnitudes of 4 or less are recorded, but not felt by many people.

Magnitudes of 6 are felt by many, break windows, and make objects move.

Magnitudes of 6.5 – 9 are major quakes, where buildings are damaged.

PROJECT

Make your own seismograph.

You will need:
three sticks about
    30 centimetres long
string and sticky tape
a soft pencil
some plasticine
some paper
a washing machine!

1. Make a tripod out of the three sticks using the sticky tape.

2. Attach the tripod to the top of the washing machine, using the plasticine.

3. Wrap the bottom end of the pencil in plasticine to make it heavier. Hang the pencil from the tripod, so it just touches the washing machine.

4. Tape some paper under the pencil.

5. Ask an adult to start the washing machine. As the washing machine runs through its cycles, the movements it makes will pass through the tripod and pencil. The pencil will record the movements on the paper. This is similar to the way a seismograph records movements within Earth.

EFFECTS OF EARTHQUAKES

Some of the biggest earthquakes occur in remote places where not many people live. They do not damage property and few people lose their lives. We usually hear about earthquakes that take place where many people live. In those places people can die, and there is great damage to buildings and homes.

Kelly, a border collie, searches buildings for survivors after the 1999 earthquake in Adapassari, Turkey.

The largest earthquake in the world is thought to have been in the Middle East in the year 1201. Using written sources from after the event, scientists have worked out that over 1 million people lost their lives.

CLEARING UP

Those still alive may be trapped in the rubble for days. Rescuers struggle to find them quickly and then get them out safely. The biggest danger to human life is often after the earthquake when help cannot get through. Fires started by broken gas pipes may rage out of control. Often the fires cannot be put out because water pipes are broken. Damaged water supplies can cause floods and, if the water is not safe to drink, diseases can spread quickly.

MIRACLE BABIES

In the 1985 earthquake in Mexico City, a tremor measuring 8.1 on the Richter scale, shook the city. More than 30,000 people were injured and at least 100,000 made homeless. Rescuers were amazed to find 14 newborn babies alive in the ruins of a hospital. Some of them had been buried for up to seven days without food or care. How did they survive?

Fire is one of the biggest dangers after an earthquake.

LIVING WITH EARTHQUAKES

All around the world, seismographs and other instruments are constantly measuring **tremors**, or shakings, in the ground. They can locate the centre of any earthquake and tell its strength. If it is going to be a big earthquake, warnings can be given to people.

People who live in earthquake zones have learned to live with the threat of earthquakes. Buildings, roads and railways are now built to stand up to earth tremors. The structures are designed to be flexible and move with the tremors. Old buildings were found to be too **rigid** and would crack apart at the first movement. Modern buildings are built in the safest areas of the city where the **bedrock** is hardest. They have rubber shock absorbers in their foundations, and their windows are designed to allow the glass to move up to 7.5 centimetres without falling out of its frame.

The 'World's Safest House' in California, USA, has been designed to resist fire and earthquakes.

PROJECT

Be an earthquake architect!

You will need:
a large marker pen
some cling film
a bowl
a packet of jelly
a small piece of paper.

1. Cover the bowl with cling film so it is as tight as a drum.

2. Place the paper on the cling film and stand the marker pen on the paper.

3. Tap the cling film lightly with your fingers.

4. Repeat steps 2 and 3 using the slab of jelly under the paper. Make sure the cling film is still tight. The jelly helps soak up the shock waves, just like earthquake-proof foundations.

Young people in earthquake zones have earthquake drills as a regular part of their school timetable. Alarms may sound if tremors over 3.5 are detected by the scientists and their seismographs.

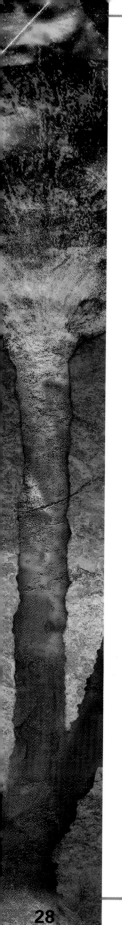

TSUNAMIS AND MUDFLOWS

Earthquakes that occur beneath the ocean floor can create huge waves that sweep across the sea. These are called **tsunamis**.

In the open ocean, a tsunami moves very fast, sometimes up to 800 kilometres (500 miles) per hour. As the wave reaches shallow water near the coast, it slows down and builds up to a giant wall of water that may be up to 30 metres high. The damage, as seen below, that occurs when a tsunami hits a seaport or harbour can be devastating.

Most tsunamis occur in the Pacific Ocean, so Hawaii is the location for the Pacific Tsunami Warning Centre, which warns coastal regions of approaching waves.

MUDFLOWS

Another after-effect of volcanoes is a **lahar**, or mudflow. This occurs when water is mixed with loose soil or volcanic ash. The water may come from heavy rain, a **crater lake** or melting snow or ice. The mudflow that is created can move as fast as a speeding car. It can travel huge distances, uprooting trees and engulfing buildings. After the **eruption** of Mount Pinatubo on the island of Luzon, in the Philippines in 1991, mudflows covered huge areas.

A lahar, or mudflow, resulting from the eruption of Mount Pinatubo in 1991.

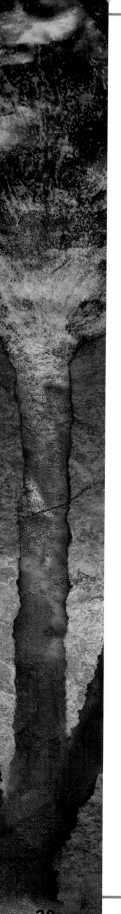

GLOSSARY

bedrock solid rock underneath an area of soil or other loose material

core central part of Earth made of iron and nickel

crater lake lake that forms in the crater of an extinct or dormant volcano

crust Earth's outer layer of rock

epicentre central point of an earthquake

erosion wearing away of rock and soil by wind and rain

erupt when lava, dust, gases or water are forced out through a weak place in Earth's crust

fault break or fracture in the rocks of Earth's crust

geothermal heat from inside Earth

lahar mudflow resulting from water mixing with volcanic ash

lava magma that reaches the surface and pours out of a volcano

magma molten (melted) rock inside Earth

mantle layer of semi-molten rock between the crust and core of Earth

plates sections of Earth's crust that move slowly about and cause changes in Earth's surface

pressure amount of force that is pressing on an area

rigid stiff and does not bend easily

seismic waves shock waves produced by an earthquake

submerged under the surface of water

tremor movement in Earth's crust

tsunami large wave produced by earthquake activity

weathering action of wind, rain and ice that cracks and breaks down rocks

FURTHER INFORMATION

BOOKS

Disasters in Nature: Earthquakes, Catherine Chambers (Heinemann Library, 2000)

Disasters in Nature: Volcanoes, Catherine Chambers (Heinemann Library, 2000)

Earthquakes, Daniel Rogers (Hodder Wayland, 2002)

Earthshock: Hurricanes, Volcanoes, Earthquakes, Tornadoes and Other Forces of Nature, Andrew Robinson (Thames and Hudson, 2002)

Nature on the Rampage: Earthquakes, Tami Deedrick (Raintree, 2003)

Nature on the Rampage: Volcanoes, Christy Steele (Raintree, 2003)

WEBSITES

Dive and Discover: Expeditions to the Seafloor – get immersed in deep-sea exploration. Read daily updates and explore towering underwater volcanoes, bizarre sea creatures and more!
http://www.divediscover.whoi.edu

Earth Observatory – view NASA satellite images of dust storms and smoke, fires, floods, storms and volcanoes.
http://earthobservatory.nasa.gov

Understanding Earthquakes – take an earthquake quiz, see earthquakes of the past 5 years positioned on a globe and learn about the history of seismology.
http://www.crustal.ucsb.edu/ics/understanding

Volcano World – everything you could want to know about volcanoes! Includes facts, pictures, video clips and currently erupting volcanoes.
http://www.volcanoworld.org

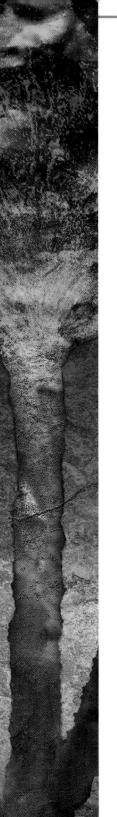

INDEX

active volcanoes 14
Andes mountains 9
ash 4, 11, 12, 17

buildings 24, 26

calderas 13
core 6, 7
craters 13
crust 7, 8

dormant volcanoes 15

earthquakes 5, 20, 21, 22, 23, 24,
    25
electricity 18, 19
epicentre 22
eruption 4, 10, 11, 12, 13
Etna, Mount 17
extinct volcanoes 15

fire 21, 25
focus 22

gases 4, 11
gemstones 19
geothermal energy 18, 19
geysers 18

hot springs 18, 19

islands 12, 13, 16, 17, 29
lahars 29
lakes 13
lava 4, 11, 17

magma 7, 10
mantle 7,
Mauna Loa 14
metals 19
mountains 9, 16, 17
mudflows 29

Pacific Ocean 8, 28
Pinatubo, Mount 12, 13, 29
plates 8

Richter scale 22
Ring of Fire 8

San Andreas fault 20, 21
San Francisco earthquake 5, 21
seismic waves 22
seismograph 22, 26, 27
seismologists 22

tidal waves 28
tremors 20
tsunamis 28

volcanoes 10, 11, 14, 15, 16, 17,
    18, 19